FAMOUS AMERICAN INDIAN LEADERS

DAKOTA BRAVE
The story of Sitting Bull

Written by: Jill C. Wheeler
Edited by: Paul J. Deegan

Published by Abdo & Daughters, 6537 Cecilia Circle, Bloomington, Minnesota 55435

Library bound edition distributed by Rockbottom Books, Pentagon Tower, P.O. Box 36036, Minneapolis, Minnesota 55435

Library of Congress Number: 89-084912   ISBN: 0-939179-67-9

Cover Photo by: Bettmann Archive
Illustrations by: Liz Dodson

A chilling night wind swept across the Dakota prairie, swirling around a tall tipi at the edge of camp. The gust snapped the hide covering the entrance, sending a stream of brisk air into the warm, smoky interior. From inside, there came a strong wail, the sound of a newborn infant making its presence known.

White Feather, the Indian midwife, stepped outside to wipe her brow. She felt secure knowing that Her Holy Door had been delivered of a healthy baby boy. Jumping Bull would be proud to learn he had a son, she thought. She turned her face up to the cloudy night sky.

Suddenly, the prairie was bathed in light. A veil of clouds had lifted from the full yellow moon. White Feather opened her eyes and stared at the silvery light. In the distance she heard the soft hoot of an owl. A smile curved across her face as she entered the tipi and went to Her Holy Door.

"The clouds no longer cover the moon, and the owl has spoken," White Feather said softly. "It is an omen — your son will be a great leader of the Sioux (SOO)."

"Hunkeshnee! (Hoon kay SHNEE)" came a cry from behind the boy. "What are you staring at? You will fall in if you get any closer."

The boy scarcely heard the warning from his friend as he stared into the depths of the icy water. "I'm looking for the water monster," he told Flying Hawk.

He had heard from the tribal elders that the water monster was rarely seen by humans. One Sioux warrior had seen it, the legend said, but he had died soon afterward, frightened to his soul by its shaggy red hair, single eye, razor-sharp horn and jagged back.

It was the right time to see it, he thought. The monster moved up the Missouri river each spring, breaking up the ice like a creeping flame.

"Hunkeshnee, come along. It is time to move camp," Flying Hawk said, turning back toward the row of tipis in the distance. "It is no wonder your name means slow," he muttered. Today the tribe was moving in search of yet another gift from Mother Earth — the buffalo.

They received much from the great shaggy beast. It provided them with meat, clothing from its hide, even tools from its bones.

But the buffalo had not always been with the Sioux. Hunkeshnee had heard the old men of the tribe tell tales of a time long ago when the Sioux people lived in a land filled with lakes and streams. Some fished and trapped for food, while others tended crops of corn, squash and beans.

Between the attacks there were long periods of peace. The leaders of the warring tribes made treaties and smoked the peace pipe.

The peace pipe, or calumet, (kal yuh MET) had been a gift from the White Buffalo Cow Maiden. She had appeared to two Sioux hunters. First she came as a beautiful woman. Then she came as a buffalo calf. Later she was a sacred white buffalo. Finally, she appeared as a dark buffalo. The calumet was made of a special stone. It was soft when newly quarried. However, it turned hard after it had been shaped into a pipe.

Sadly, the calumet could not guarantee peace. Eventually, the Sioux were forced from their wooded lands by stronger Indian tribes. They moved to the vast prairies. That is where they now lived in harmony with the Great Spirit and the plentiful buffalo.

Hunkeshnee's mind was full of thoughts of the upcoming buffalo hunt as he set out to explore his new surroundings. He was in his tenth summer, and while he knew he had the strength and skill needed to join the hunt, he still was considered too young.

After a while, Hunkeshnee and his friends left to explore new surroundings. Later they stopped to rest on a bluff overlooking a river valley. In the distance, the buffalo herd grazed contentedly. The shaggy animals looked peaceful and harmless from this distance, but Hunkeshnee knew of more than one brave who had fallen under the thundering hooves. And tomorrow his tribe would send out a hunting party for a buffalo hunt.

"Tomorrow I will kill my first buffalo," Hunkeshnee said suddenly.

"You?" Little Arrow questioned. "You are only in your 10th summer. You are barely big enough to ride your pony. How can you conquer the mighty buffalo?"

"You will see," Hunkeshnee said, still staring at the scene below him. "I have a plan."

The next day dawned warm and clear. The hunting party was up at the first light. The braves who had been selected by the chief the night before mounted their horses. They began riding toward the herd. They took turns shooting arrows straight ahead. This was done to make certain they followed a straight path. They would do the same on the way back to camp. This kept them from getting lost on the endless, windswept prairie.

Back at camp, Hunkeshnee was waiting. He had crept out of the tipi and had escaped the watchful eyes of the tribal police guarding the camp. Now he was hidden behind a small cliff, out of sight of the hunters.

Hunkeshnee knew the hunters would circle the herd while remaining far enough away to avoid being detected. When the call came, they would surge down upon the herd, each brave matching strength and skill with the mighty creatures in the ultimate battle of the plains.

Suddenly, Hunkeshnee saw the first of the braves riding for the herd as fast as he could. With a cry, Hunkeshnee dug his heels into the pony's side and bent his head into the wind, heading right for the center of the herd.

The buffalo had been caught off guard. The animals began to run in all directions, and each hunter picked one out and kept it in his sight.

Hunkeshnee had spotted a bull. A giant, shaggy creature, it must have stood six feet high. Hunkeshnee rode within several yards of the mighty animal. He fitted his arrow to his strong bow and took aim for the spot just to the left of the bull's heart. The arrow hit its mark, and the bull snorted in pain. It slowed its pace and turned to look at its attacker.

The Indian boy drew in his pony. He reached for another arrow. The buffalo pawed the ground, preparing to charge. The sight of the heaving, snorting animal made Hunkeshnee's pony suddenly rear. The quick movement threw the Indian boy onto the ground. The pony danced away in fear as Hunkeshnee struggled to get to his feet. The bull's black eyes glared at him, and the animal lowered his head to charge.

Hunkeshnee aiming his second arrow at the buffalo.

Hunkeshnee never before had felt so afraid. He clenched his teeth and aimed a second arrow. If it didn't hit its mark, he would have little chance of escaping. He drew a deep breath and let the arrow fly. The stone point landed in the animal's chest. The bull jerked in pain.

The move gave Hunkeshnee enough time to run and jump on his pony. It was ready because it had been trained never to leave its master. He whirled his mount around in time to see the bull charging him. However, Hunkeshnee and the pony were able to dodge the wounded animal, which fell to the ground.

"It is Hunkeshnee! He has killed the first buffalo?" came a cry from behind. Hunkeshnee turned to see Black Dog, one of the braves who had been chosen for the hunt.

Hunkeshnee proudly walked over to the fallen beast. Tonight there would be a feast to celebrate his accomplishments. All feats were honored in this way, and all heroics recounted for the entire tribe. In such a way was the history of the tribe kept alive.

Sitting Bull was tired. He was hunting near camp, but the rabbits he sought were nowhere in sight. The heat of the prairie was stifling. He made his way over to a shady tree and sat on the ground, wiping his brow.

He was now in his 14th year and already considered a man, having killed a buffalo and counted coup in a raid on a band of Crows, old enemies of the Sioux.

Counting coup was the greatest honor a Sioux warrior could earn. It involved striking an enemy, whether with a hand, a weapon or a special coup stick, usually made of bone. For his feat of bravery, he had been given his adult name. Now, rather than playing with bows and arrows, Sitting Bull was expected to use them to help feed the tribe.

The shifting grasses and gentle songs of the Bird People were soothing. Sitting Bull soon fell asleep.

"Be still?"

Sitting Bull awoke instantly, but did not open his eyes.

"Be still!"

The unspoken words came into his mind again as he lay motionless. Then he heard it — a rustling in the grass nearby. He trained his other senses on the environment around him, searching for clues as to what the words had meant.

Then he smelled it. The strong, choking smell of a grizzly bear! He kept his eyes closed and his body perfectly still as he felt the bear amble near him. The huge, shaggy beast sniffed him, sending a gust of warm breath over Sitting Bull's bare shoulder. Still he didn't move.

The huge grizzly nudged him gently with his giant paw. Seeing no motion, it moved off again across the prairie. Sitting Bull waited several moments before looking to make sure the beast was gone.

He drew a deep breath and sat up, scanning the branches above him to find the spirit which had saved his life. He knew all objects had a spirit — rocks and trees, birds and animals, too. The spirits could change form, just as they could send visions and messages.

He found his lifesaving spirit perched high above him. It was in the form of a tiny bird which was watching him carefully with bright brown eyes.

Sitting Bull was told to be still by a Spirit as a grizzly approached.

13

"Thank you, my little friend," he said out loud. "You are indeed the closest of the animals to the Great Spirit."

Sitting Bull stood up to go back to camp, his heart light. The Bird People had favored him! By sparing his life, they had shown him that he was to be a great leader. He knew it was time to prepare for his new role by seeking a vision from his guardian spirit.

The train of covered wagons creaked and swayed its way across the endless prairie. From a bluff above, Chief Sitting Bull, watched the white settlers. They seemed to move ever westward into land which once had been the Indians' alone.

The white men had promised that the country was to be for the Indians. They had even signed an agreement stating that no white settlers would be allowed on the land, even if they were only passing through it.

But the promise had been broken, just as so many other white men's promises had crumbled in the past years.

Many of the other tribes had given in to the white man's wishes and moved to reservations. Sitting Bull refused to strand his people there. They were a proud people, a people of the plains. They would, Sitting Bull decreed, live off the gifts of the Great Spirit and the buffalo. They were not going to live off handouts of the white man.

It was the greatest gathering of Sioux Indians in many years. They had come from across the plains — Sitting Bull's tribe, the Hunkpapas, along with the Cheyennes (Shy AN), the Minneconjous (Mi ni con JOUS), the Oglalas (Ah GLAH la) and others. The huge Indian camp sprawled along the banks of Rosebud Creek for nearly three miles.

All along the river bank there were noises of joyous reunions. Laughter and sounds of celebrations came from among the nearly 15,000 Indians who had gathered there. The gathering was a time to make laws and treaties among themselves. There also was time to visit. And the young men and women of the different tribes could get to know each other. Then they could marry, as was the custom among Sioux tribes.

The exception to the celebrations was in Sitting Bull's tent. The scouts had brought him bad news. The white man's army was gathering nearby. The white man meant to force him and his people to reservations. That much he knew. He did not want to fight. But fighting was his only alternative to the prison of a reservation.

"We are surrounded," Sitting Bull told the war council that evening. "The white man is around us and if we do not work together we shall be torn apart."

He gazed solemnly at the chief's sitting around the fire in front of him. There were the other Hunkpapa chiefs — Gall, Crow King and Black Moon. The great Oglala warrior Crazy Horse had taken over the leadership of his people. He was

A scout telling Sitting Bull they were surrounded by the white man.

there with Low Dog and Big Road. Two Moon and White Bull were there representing the northern Cheyennes. Together they formed a circle of strength. But would it be enough to save their land and their people from the white man's invasion?

The flicker of the firelight cast dancing shadows on his rugged face. "The white man wants war. We shall give it to him."

For the next week, the camp prepared for war. Sitting Bull and the other leaders had sent all of the women and children to a safe place. They were hidden away in the mountains. Now, the men concentrated on getting ready for a battle.

For the Sioux, strength came from the Sun Dance, a sacred ceremony given to the people by an ancient man named Kablaya (Kah BLAH ya). Kablaya had learned the dance from a dream, and he gave it to the Sioux to restore their power.

The final step before beginning the dance was purification in the sweat lodge. And as the sun rose, the dance began.

Sitting Bull steeled himself for the pain. It was part of the dance — just as it had been when Kablaya offered two pieces of his flesh in the first Sun Dance. The chief's face was void of emotion as a warrior sliced fifty small cuts in each of his arms, from wrist to shoulder. With the warm, sticky blood running down his arms, the Hunkpapa chief stood up slowly and began moving to the deepening beat of the drums.

For two days he danced, taking neither food nor water. His movements grew slower, his steps weaker. On the afternoon of the second day, the sun grew black. Then he collapsed on the sandy floor of the lodge. The blackness dissolved into the mist of a dream.

He was looking down upon a large Indian camp. As he watched, he saw thousands of the white man's soldiers tumbling head over heels from the sky. They fell into the camp, their blue uniforms shadowed against the prairie sky.

There would be a war, and the Indians would be victorious! The camp was buzzing over the revelations from Sitting Bull's Sun Dance vision.

Shortly thereafter, a band of Sioux and Cheyenne warriors led by Crazy Horse stopped a column of white soldiers on Rosebud Creek. After the victory, the giant Indian camp moved to a new site on the banks of the Little Big Horn. One week later, on June 25, 1876, the white man's army arrived. The time for war had come.

"Soldiers coming! Soldiers coming!"

A band of Cheyenne, Hunkpapa and Lakota warriors were the first to reach the soldiers. They began their assault by killing the Indian scouts which the whites had employed to lead them to Sitting Bull's camp. The soldiers, frightened by the huge number of warriors, jumped down to fight on foot. But on foot they were a poor match for the quick, agile Indians who relied on skill and strength rather than many guns and bullets.

In minutes, the white soldiers broke ranks and began racing for a patch of brush and trees near the river. The warriors cut them down one by one.

The Indians battling General Custer at the battle of Little Big Horn.

20

The battle was soon over, and Sitting Bull's vision was proven correct by the sight which remained when the smoke and dust settled. The grassy hillside where the battle had taken place was now littered with blue uniforms, just like in his vision. More than 200 white soldiers lay dead, struck down by his brave warriors.

The sound of a band of horsemen filtered through the cool spring air near Sitting Bull's camp. The chief stood up quickly — the hunters had returned! His hungry people would soon be able to get their fill of the rich, savory buffalo meat.

His heart sank as he stepped outside to meet the hunting party. They had returned empty handed, and with them was a riderless horse.

"We saw no buffalo," said Crooked Tree, who had led the hunting party. "The white man has driven them away."

Buffalo had been scarce ever since the tribe had moved to Canada four years ago. Sitting Bull had made the journey to escape the anger of the white man. After the Sioux victory over General Custer at the Little Big Horn, Sitting Bull was a wanted man.

Back across the border in the United States, the whites continued moving ever westward. Their presence sealed the legendary cave from which the buffalo emerged each spring.

"I have had enough," Sitting Bull said. "My people are starving. There is no hope for the red man now. We have no choice but to surrender."

"Send a messenger to the white soldiers," he told the warrior. "Ask them what they want from us so that we may finally live in peace."

Sitting Bull smiled gently at his son, Crowfoot. He had recently been reunited with his family after spending several years as a prisoner of war at Fort Randall. He was glad to be back with the young brave, even if their home was now a reservation called Standing Rock in what would become North Dakota.

After two years in captivity, the aging chief was beginning to accept the white man. He had even tried to teach some of them how to speak Dakota. He found they were much like Indians — some were honest, and others could not be trusted.

As the pair approached their tipi, Sitting Bull saw a crowd had gathered. At the center of the group was a young white man with long dark hair and a wide mustache. He was dressed in a brightly decorated buckskin jacket and leggings, with shiny holsters on either hip.

". . . the great Indian nation," Sitting Bull heard him say. "Where do I find the man who brought George Custer to his knees?"

"Who do you seek," Sitting Bull called to him as he approached.

"I seek the slayer of Custer, Sitting Bull, the great leader of the Sioux," the young man said. "Do you know where I might find him?"

"You have found him," the Indian said slowly. "I am Sitting Bull."

24

"I am honored to meet you," the young man said, bowing deeply. "Your bravery is well known. I am Buffalo Bill Cody. I have come to ask if you would do me the honor of appearing in my Wild West Show. Many people would like to see you and hear your tales of the Indian wars."

Sitting Bull was silent for a moment. There was something appealing about the idea of joining the charming young man, of leaving the confines of Standing Rock. Perhaps he would be able to learn even more about the white culture and grow to understand them.

"I will do it," he said finally.

For one season, Sitting Bull traveled with the Wild West Show. He became the star attraction, and after each show, the people would crowd around him and ask for his autograph. He learned to sign his name in English for the curious fans, and he sent the money he earned back to his tribe at Standing Rock.

After the show closed, he traveled with the show to Washington, D.C., where he was introduced to President Grover Cleveland.

The past few years had brought scorching droughts and howling blizzards to the reservations. These left the Indians cold and hungry. At the same time, the federal government had been cutting back on the Indians' rations. The government hoped to force them to produce their own food. However, the Indians had no tools or implements with which to do so.

Many Indian children had died when their undernourished bodies were ravaged by diseases. Measles and whooping cough were killers. The children had no resistance to these diseases. They had been unknown among the Indians before the white man's arrival.

The sense of despair grew deeper on the reservation. The feeling of hopelessness had encouraged a new religion. This belief rolled over the plains like a summer storm.

Believers sought a sign from Wovoka, who had been a Paiute medicine man. They thought he would show them how to return to paradise. Soon the plains would be full of buffalo once again.

The reservation was named after the Legend of Standing Rock; a Indian princess who turned to stone.

The white man would leave and Indian leaders would rise from the dead.

Believers thougth Wovoka had gone to heaven when he had had a vision — a vision of a ghost dance. Now if they too did the dance, paradise would return.

Thus, the mournful, wailing sounds of the Ghost Dance grew in intensity on reservations across the prairie. But no visions came.

However, the authorities heard about the dance. They became alarmed. More soldiers were sent to the reservations. They believed the old Hunkpapa chief was at the heart of the movement. Reservation officials were quick to order Sitting Bull's arrest.

Sitting Bull was awakened by a loud crash as the door to his cabin was thrown open. He heard footsteps coming toward him. Rough hands shook him and pulled him from his bed.

"I'm holding you prisoner," said the intruder. Sitting Bull recognized him as an Indian named Bullhead, who worked as a policeman on the reservation. Bullhead motioned to the other Indian policemen to take the old chief out to their waiting ponies.

Sitting Bull began to fight, but he was outnumbered by the three men holding him down. They dragged him outside into the frosty air. Seeing that no one from his tribe was around, Sitting Bull took a deep breath and uttered a war cry.

The cry brought his followers rushing out of their tents and cabins. When they saw what was happening, they crowded around the struggling chief.

"I'm not going!" Sitting Bull yelled. "Do what you like with me, but I'm not going!"

Suddenly, the air was split by a gunshot. The Indian police grabbed their weapons and began firing into the crowd. Sitting Bull slumped to the ground, shot dead.

The mighty warrior who had survived so many battles with the white man had been killed at the hands of his own people.

Meanwhile, Indians and police fell to the ground. Those left standing after the firing ended ran to the nearby cabins for shelter. After more soldiers arrived, the policemen began searching through the cabins. They broke windows and stole whatever valuables they found. They also slaughtered the tribe's livestock and left the bodies to freeze in the winter cold.

When the looting was done, the police loaded their dead into a wagon to return them to the fort. One of their leaders was Red Tomahawk. He insisted that they load Sitting Bull's body as well. He said he had been given orders that the chief was to be brought back, dead or alive.

Grumbling, the police heaved Sitting Bull's shattered body into the wagon and took off for the fort.

The wagon rumbled off into the distance. The morning sun sparkled brightly on the blood-stained snow.